Just Dance

Modern Dance

Wendy Hinote Lanier
and Madeline Nixon

AV2
www.av2books.com

Step 1
Go to www.av2books.com

Step 2
Enter this unique code

JZDAKKZLW

Step 3
Explore your interactive eBook!

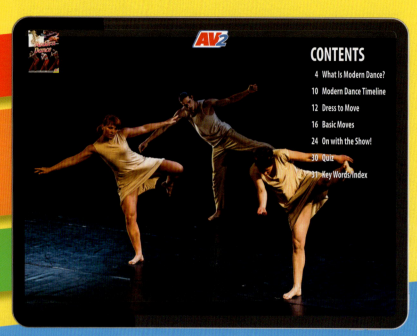

AV2 is optimized for use on any device

Your interactive eBook comes with...

Contents
Browse a live contents page to easily navigate through resources

Audio
Listen to sections of the book read aloud

Videos
Watch informative video clips

Weblinks
Gain additional information for research

Try This!
Complete activities and hands-on experiments

Key Words
Study vocabulary, and complete a matching word activity

Quizzes
Test your knowledge

Slideshows
View images and captions

... and much, much more!

Modern Dance

Contents

AV2 Book Code   2

Chapter 1
What Is Modern Dance?   4
Modern Dance Timeline   10

Chapter 2
Dress to Move   12

Chapter 3
Basic Moves   16

Chapter 4
On with the Show!   24
Quiz   30
Key Words/Index   31

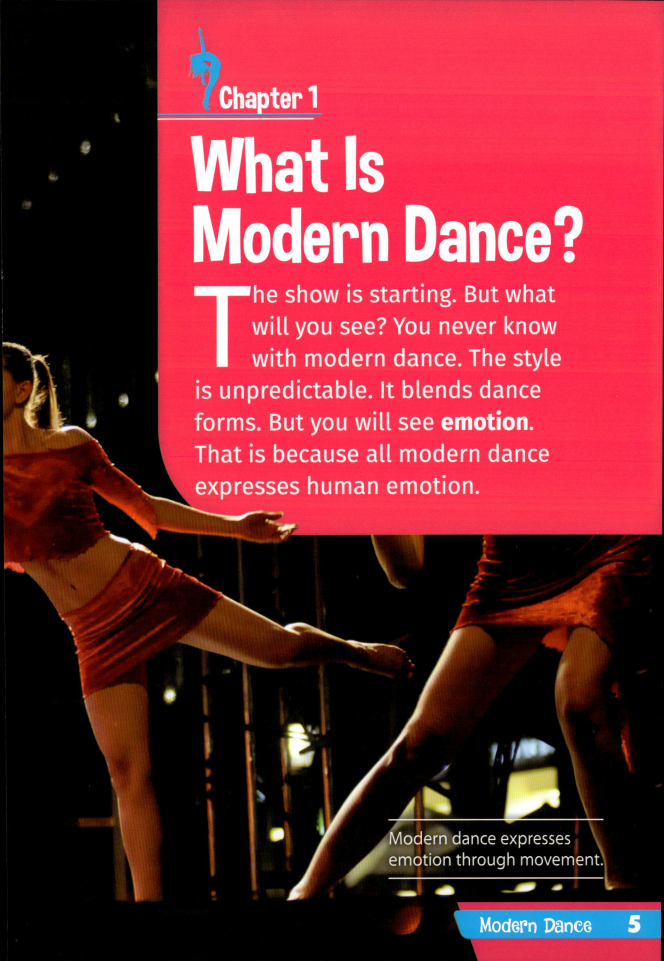

Chapter 1

What Is Modern Dance?

The show is starting. But what will you see? You never know with modern dance. The style is unpredictable. It blends dance forms. But you will see **emotion**. That is because all modern dance expresses human emotion.

Modern dance expresses emotion through movement.

Modern dance began in the early 1900s. It was meant to be different from ballet. Classical ballet is very **structured**. Modern dance is not. Early modern dance leaders stressed free movement. Personal experiences were important, too. Dancers used their bodies as instruments. Their bodies showed emotions such as joy or fear. Many movements were close to the floor. In some moves, dancers were almost **horizontal**. Dances often included falling.

Dance Tip

Do not plan your movements. Instead, listen to the music. Let your movements take you wherever the music leads.

Modern dance uses movements from other dancing styles, such as ballet.

Modern Dance 7

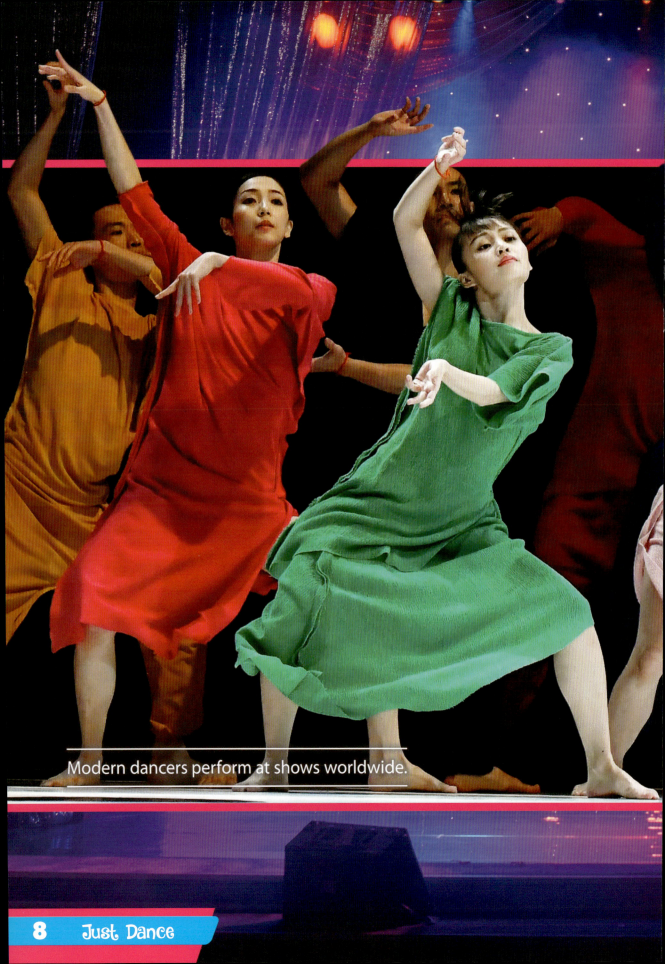

Modern dancers perform at shows worldwide.

Modern dance is still growing. Some ballet movements are still used. But today's **choreography** shows other forms. Dancers also bring their own styles. This is changing the way we define modern dance.

Modern dance is the **FOURTH MOST POPULAR** dance style in the United States.

In **1933**, Ted Shawn founded the first all male modern dance group, *Ted Shawn and His Men Dancers*.

Modern Dance Timeline

Modern dance has always been closely linked with emotions and feelings. It started as a break from ballet's strict rules. Dance moves borrow from ballet, but take more risks. Later, modern dance grew to include movement from many different dance styles.

1902

Loie Fuller and Isadora Duncan tour Europe together. They take chances with creative stage lighting, costumes, and movement.

1915

Ruth St. Denis and Ted Shawn, two of the first modern dance teachers, open the Denishawn School of Dancing and Related Arts.

1926

Modern dance pioneer Martha Graham founds the Martha Graham Dance Company in New York.

Costume, light, music, and movement are all choices and additions that make modern dance strong.

1946

José Limón opens the José Limón Dance Company with former Denishawn instructor, Doris Humphrey. Here, he creates the Limón technique which focuses on breath and body weight while dancing and is still used today.

1958

Alvin Ailey opens the Alvin Ailey American Dance Theatre. He uses modern dance to focus on the African-American experience. The company becomes one of the most successful dance companies in the world.

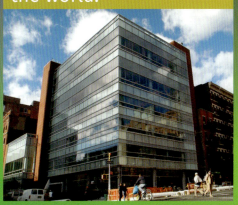

Today

Today, modern dance teachers encourage students to study choreography and **kinesiology**. Several colleges offer joint dance and kinesiology programs. Studying kinesiology helps modern dancers understand their body movements better and prevent injury.

Modern Dance 11

Modern dancers dress in costumes that reflect the mood of the dance.

Chapter 2

Dress to Move

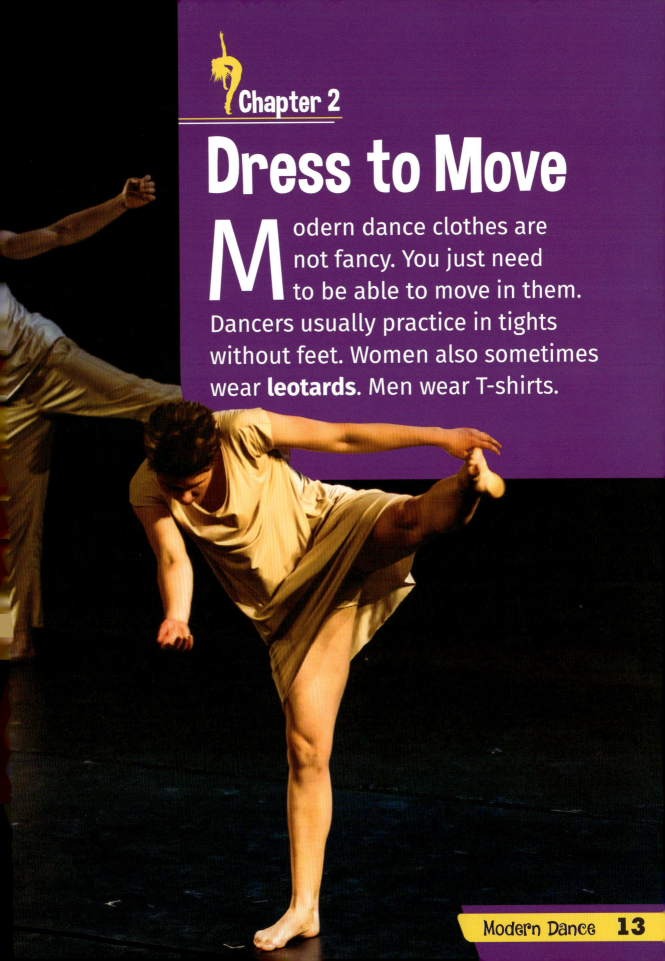

Modern dance clothes are not fancy. You just need to be able to move in them. Dancers usually practice in tights without feet. Women also sometimes wear **leotards**. Men wear T-shirts.

Performance clothes are simple, too. Dancers aim to express emotion. Clothes should help do this.

Clothes do not draw attention. The audience should focus on the movements. Women often wear thin, flowing dresses. Their arms and legs are bare. Men usually wear tights and a shirt.

Most modern dancers perform barefoot. But some wear shoes. They sometimes choose leather or canvas ballet slippers.

Dance Tip

You might feel uncomfortable while dancing. Take a deep breath and stay focused.

Bare feet allow dancers to feel the floor.

Modern Dance 15

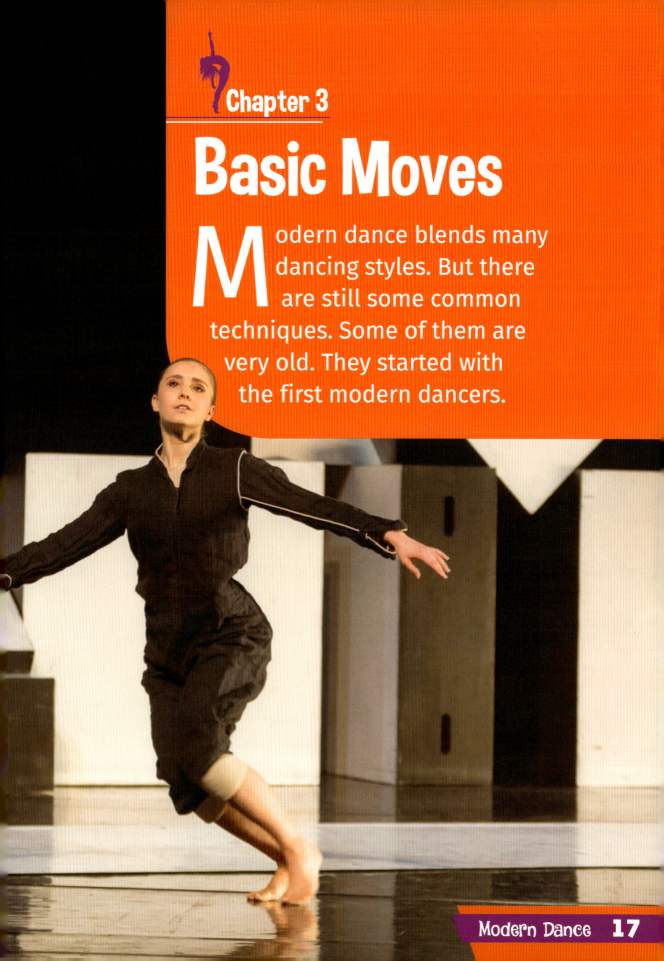

Chapter 3

Basic Moves

Modern dance blends many dancing styles. But there are still some common techniques. Some of them are very old. They started with the first modern dancers.

One is the Graham technique. It is named after Martha Graham. The move is based on **contraction** and release. The contraction happens in your stomach. First, exhale while tightening your stomach muscles. This creates an inward curve to the body. Next, release your stomach muscles when you inhale. Then lengthen your stomach. Finally, return to an upright position.

Dance Tip

Modern dance pushes your body to its limits. Warm up by stretching. It helps you avoid injury.

Modern dancers use their body weight to make dramatic movements.

Modern Dance 19

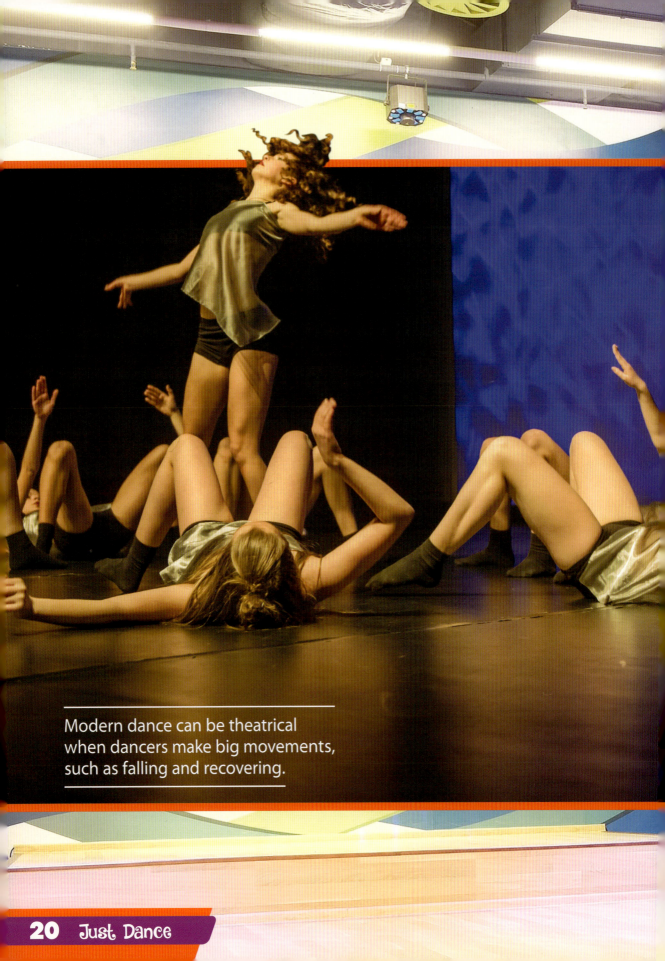

Modern dance can be theatrical when dancers make big movements, such as falling and recovering.

The Humphrey technique is also old. Doris Humphrey created it. She had a belief that all movement was somewhere between balance and falling. Her technique shows this. It is based on the body's reaction to falling. In this technique, dancers push the limits of their balance. They do a controlled fall. But they recover their balance.

Dance Tip

Do not be afraid to copy movements from other dancers. Do you see a movement that looks good? Try it for yourself.

Try It Out

Express Yourself

Think of an idea or event that creates a strong feeling in you. The feeling might be anger or joy. It might be sadness or fear. Or it might be some other emotion. Now try to express that feeling to others with only your movements.

There are no set patterns in modern dance. You can express yourself in any way you like. You can use music. But you do not have to.

Modern dancers follow the routines created by choreographers.

Chapter 4
On with the Show!

Modern dancers communicate through movement. This movement must be seen to be understood. That is why modern dance is often performed for an audience.

Many top dancers work with **companies**. Some **specialize** in modern dance. These dancers are well trained. They have practiced all the major dance styles. And they perform wherever there is space. Sometimes, it is in a theater. But it could be anywhere, such as a park.

There are other ways to see a modern dance performance. You might watch one on television. Or you can find videos online.

Dance Tip

Try to keep your weight balanced on the balls of your feet. This allows you to move quickly and smoothly.

In some performances, modern dancers work together.

Modern Dance 27

The best dancers are picked for a company. But all dancers must start with the basics. Your body must be trained. It must also be **disciplined**. Use warm-up exercises. Use dance techniques. Use movement patterns, too. After years of study, you can **audition** for a company. Who knows? You may turn out to be a modern dance star!

The Paul Taylor Dance Company opened in **1954** and is **ONE OF THE LONGEST RUNNING** modern dance companies in the United Sates.

Most modern dancers practice **FOUR TIMES A WEEK**.

Professional dance companies showcase the best of modern dancing.

Modern Dance 29

Quiz

1. What is the goal of modern dance?
2. Why do modern dancers typically not wear elaborate costumes?
3. What does keeping your weight on the balls of your feet do?
4. What is the Humphrey technique?
5. Why did modern dance begin in the 1900s?
6. What do modern dance teachers encourage students to study today?
7. Why do modern dancers usually not wear shoes?
8. Who are two dancers that began experimenting with light and costume?
9. What is the Graham technique?
10. What do men wear to modern dance?

ANSWERS

1. To express human emotion 2. They do not want to limit their motion. 3. Allows quick and smooth movement 4. Controlled falling 5. To break from ballet 6. Choreography and kinesiology 7. To feel the floor 8. Loie Fuller and Isadora Duncan 9. Contraction and release 10. T-shirts

Key Words

audition to give a short performance as a test

choreography the arrangement of steps and movements for a dance

companies groups of professional dancers

contraction the tensing of a muscle

disciplined the ability to make oneself do the right thing

emotion a state of feeling

horizontal flat or parallel to the ground

kinesiology the study of how the body moves

leotards form-fitting one-piece clothes usually worn by dancers

specialize to be involved in or participate in a particular type of activity

structured made up of certain types of steps and movements

Index

audition 28, 31

ballet 4, 9, 10, 14, 30

choreography 9, 11, 30, 31
companies 11, 26, 28, 29, 31

Duncan, Isadora 10, 30

emotions 5, 6, 10, 14, 22, 30, 31

falling 6, 20, 21, 30
Fuller, Loie 10, 30

Graham, Martha 10, 18
Graham technique 18, 30

Humphrey, Doris 11, 21
Humphrey technique 21, 30

Limón, José 11

performance clothes 13, 14, 31

Shawn, Ted 9, 10

Modern Dance 31

Get the best of both worlds.

AV2 bridges the gap between print and digital.

The expandable resources toolbar enables quick access to content including **videos**, **audio**, **activities**, **weblinks**, **slideshows**, **quizzes**, and **key words**.

Animated videos make static images come alive.

Resource icons on each page help readers to further **explore key concepts**.

Published by AV2
350 5th Avenue, 59th Floor
New York, NY 10118
Website: www.av2books.com

Copyright © 2021 AV2
All rights reserved. No part of this publication may be reproduced, stored in a retrieval system, or transmitted in any form or by any means, electronic, mechanical, photocopying, recording, or otherwise, without the prior written permission of the publisher.

Library of Congress Cataloging-in-Publication Data
Names: Lanier, Wendy Hinote, author.
Title: Modern dance / Wendy Hinote Lanier and Madeline Nixon.
Description: New York, NY : AV2, 2021. | Series: Just dance | Includes index. | Audience: Ages 8-12 | Audience: Grades 4-6
Identifiers: LCCN 2019058811 (print) | LCCN 2019058812 (ebook) | ISBN 9781791123321 (library binding) | ISBN 9781791123338 (paperback) | ISBN 9781791123345 | ISBN 9781791123352
Subjects: LCSH: Modern dance--Juvenile literature.
Classification: LCC GV1783 .L38 2021 (print) | LCC GV1783 (ebook) | DDC 792.8--dc23
LC record available at https://lccn.loc.gov/2019058811
LC ebook record available at https://lccn.loc.gov/2019058812

Printed in Guangzhou, China
1 2 3 4 5 6 7 8 9 0 24 23 22 21 20

022020
101319

Project Coordinator: Heather Kissock   Designer: Ana María Vidal

Every reasonable effort has been made to trace ownership and to obtain permission to reprint copyright material. The publishers would be pleased to have any errors or omissions brought to their attention so that they may be corrected in subsequent printings.

Weigl acknowledges Getty Images, Alamy, and Shutterstock as its primary image suppliers for this title.

First published by North Star Editions in 2018.